Whose Report Will You Believe?

by

Marilyn Phillipps

Cover by Debra Wilson, 1993.

Acknowledgments

My sincere thanks to my husband Michael, who encouraged me to finally finish this book. His love and support have made our ministry together possible and his indipensable vision keeps us on track and filled with faith. Every event recounted in this book was absolutely worth it when I see what the Lord is doing in us and through us today! I am so thankful the Lord would not let me give up! His plan is wonderous!

Introduction

Praise be to the God and Father of our Lord Jesus Christ, the Father of compassion and the God of all comfort who comforts us in all our troubles so that we can comfort those who are in trouble with the comfort we ourselves have received from God. 2 Corinthians 1:3,4

May this book share with you the comfort the Lord has given me and the victory that He has achieved.

Our marriage was in such trouble that after one session with a marriage counselor, he told us he couldn't help us. "There's nothing that can be done for this marriage," he said. "You're wasting your money coming here. You should get a quick divorce, get it over with and go on with life."

I then went to our pastor who said, "Sometimes when things have gone this far, it's best just to get a divorce." I know what it feels like to be facing impossible circumstances and be unable to find someone who will tell you it can be done. The Lord is reaching out to those who have no hope.

There is hope in Jesus. There is healing in Jesus. There is victory in Jesus!

In The Beginning

Michael and I were born and raised in homes filled with religious fervor. Although there have been things in our backgrounds that we have had to overcome, we praise God for our upbringing. Our parents taught us to be faithful and obedient. We learned a faithfulness that the Lord used later in our lives.

Our fathers were both in the military and our families traveled within the United States and abroad. In the 1950's our dads were both stationed in Denver and Michael and I probably even played together at the Lowry AFB Nursery. We don't know that for sure but we could have.

We didn't meet officially until 1967, when we were juniors in college in Denver. I was a nursing student at Loretto Heights College and Michael was attending the University of Colorado. Our mothers met at a church retreat and immediately wanted the two of us to meet each other. I don't know if you ever met any daughters or sons of your mother's friends, but I had one experience like that and I didn't want to repeat it. So when my mother said she wanted me to meet her new friend's son, I tried to ignore her suggestion. Michael did the same thing, so it was about four or five months from the time our mothers met until we did.

I can't tell you it was love at first sight. Actually, we couldn't stand each other. Michael thought there were a lot of things about me that needed to be changed and he told me what they were within five minutes of our introduction. I thought he was arrogant. So we parted ways and didn't see each other for a matter of months.

Michael traveled to Canada to Expo '67 and when he came back he called me. Perhaps God had His hand on us then because I really had no idea what prompted Michael to call me or me to go out with him, but our second encounter proved better than our first.

We went out for several months, but our relationship was very stormy. After each date we would resolve never to see each other again. We had a very competitive relationship though, and each one of us refused to let the other one get the upper hand. So we continued to see each other for a matter of months until finally we decided that we had better things to do in life and parted ways. It was at that time of separation that we discovered that we had fallen in love with each other. How that ever happened neither of us knew.

The Navy paid for the last two years of my education, so when I graduated in 1969 I owed them three years service. Michael still had one year of college left because he had changed his major. When I left for basic training, we were planning to be married sometime in the next year or so.

I had attended an all-girl denominational college and was totally unprepared for what I faced out in the world. While in basic training, I was introduced to a doctor ten years my senior. I went out to dinner with him on our first date and he told me he was divorced.

My whole background said you don't date divorced men but I figured what's one dinner. Well, it was one dinner and another dinner and another dinner and pretty soon I was seeing him every day. Before I knew it, I was very involved with him.

Now, in looking back, I can see I was a young girl and he was a very sophisticated man of the world. At the time, though, I really felt I was in love with him. So I wrote to Michael and told him that I had found someone else and I was breaking off our engagement.

When I arrived at my first assignment in California two months later, my doctor was supposed to come out to meet me. I waited and I waited but I didn't hear from him for a month. Finally he called me one day and said, "I didn't know how to tell you this, but I'm not really divorced."

I was completely disillusioned. I had fallen in love with a married man. It was my first experience dealing with the world and it hurt more than I could express. I had really trusted, and I had been betrayed. Yet God had His hand on me even then. He was trying to reach me, but I wasn't listening.

The next few months were a blur to me. Between the regimentation of the Navy and the death of my dreams of love, I just lost contact with reality. I wandered to work every day and wandered back. I was faced with all kinds of dating pressures that I had never experienced before in my life.

Everybody lived such a fast-paced life. Excessive drinking and sexual sin seemed to be the standard. I seemed to have lost my anchor and I was standing on shifting sand.

Then a young Marine who was being dishonorably

discharged was confined to our medical ward on house arrest while awaiting his final hearing. We spent many hours talking and I got to know him well. He was a very easy-going hippie type and I really liked his lifestyle. It was quite a contrast from rigors of military life.

When he was released, he moved to a commune with a group of people who were very heavy into drugs. I spent a lot of time at his house, but I was never involved in the drug scene. I just enjoyed watching those people interact, amazed by their love for each other.

I became very infatuated with their kind of life. They shared their food, their paychecks, and everything they had in common. I saw a real love there that I hadn't seen in the world and I decided there was something really good going on there.

In the midst of my confusion and all those circumstances, I took advantage of a four-day weekend and flew home. Someone who knew Michael told him I was in town and he called me up and said he'd like to see me. I didn't think it was such a great idea but I agreed to meet.

As the time grew closer for our meeting, though, my heart started pounding with excitement. When I woke up that morning and realized Michael was coming over, I couldn't wait to see him. By the time he got there, I knew I was deeply in love with him and, unfortunately, I had made quite a mess of things.

The Early Years

We got engaged again. Finally my life seemed to be making some sense and I felt things stabilizing. That was in October 1969 and in January 1970 I flew back to Colorado for our wedding. We had a nine-day honeymoon and then I flew back to work in California. Michael returned to school in Boulder to finish up his senior year.

About a month later, I experienced what I thought was the flu, but I couldn't seem to get over it. I was working nights and was worn out so I suspected that was the reason for my constant nausea. When I went to sick call, however, I found out that my "flu" was really a baby. When I called Michael and told him I was pregnant, he said, "You're WHAT?"

We had a lot of long-term plans, one of which was to make a lot of money. Now we faced a new development that might curtail all those dreams. We were in shock. Now I see God's wisdom in sending a baby our way immediately. If He hadn't, we'd might never have had one. We were so concentrating on the world and materialistic gain.

Since I was pregnant back before they allowed women to have babies and stay in the service, they very quickly ushered me out and I moved back to Denver.

Michael graduated from college and we moved to his first job with a chemical company in a small town in the Midwest. He immediately threw himself into becoming the ultimate corporate executive. I painted and decorated and filled our empty house with large amounts of garage-sale furniture. Before we knew it, our beautiful baby Cristine was born. We hardly even knew each other and already we had a baby.

That first year in corporate America introduced us to the cocktail circuit. We learned it was important to attend just the right parties and to throw good ones in return, and we became very good at both.

Neither one of us knew the Lord. We didn't have a Rock to stand on. All we had was the ritual of the church that we attended regularly. Because we didn't know Jesus, we filled our days with many activities but our lives were empty.

When Cristine was three months old I went back to work. With the two of us working, our income increased greatly and we were able to buy more things. We filled our home with many expensive items, but our lives were still empty. One day Michael announced, "I want to go back to Denver." It sounded fine to me.

He quit his corporate job and I quit my nursing position. We packed up and moved back to Denver with absolutely no plans for our future. We moved into a small and dingy basement apartment. Michael found a job laying tennis courts and I got a part-time nursing job. The money was slim, but we still managed to acquire more "stuff."

One day about a year later, Michael decided he wanted to invent, so he quit his job. Throughout the year we had been drifting apart so when he made his announcement it hardly mattered to me what he did. (I thought at that time that we were far apart, but we had even farther to go.)

I said, "Fine, you invent, if I can have a baby." Michael didn't particularly want another child, but it was a good trade-off, so he agreed.

I got pregnant again and had to go to work full-time since Michael was not working. I was on call for OB patients every other day for twenty-four hour shifts. I was called in to work at all hours of the day and night—whatever time my patients went into labor—and I stayed at the hospital until they delivered. Michael and I never saw each other, we just left messages like, "Hi, there's a sandwich in the fridge" or "I'll be home late tonight."

I started maternity leave on a Friday and Mike, Jr. was born the following Monday. I was home for six weeks maternity leave and went right back to work again. I pumped milk while I worked at night so that the sitter could feed our baby during the day and then I pumped milk in between naps during the day so that Michael could feed him at night. I hardly ever actually saw our baby.

I begin to realize I was on a treadmill—trying to take care of the house, trying to take care of babies, trying to juggle a career. Every spare moment I had I threw myself into the children because I felt so guilty about leaving them. Michael's needs came at the bottom of my list of priorities. I only had so much energy and I usually ran out long before I got to him. Finally I decided the only way to get off the treadmill was to go to graduate school. That way I could further my career and wouldn't have to work for a while.

Michael and I never discussed anything so one day I just announced, "You better get a job. I'm going to quit work." By that time his desire to invent had lost its appeal so he agreed.

He got a job selling homes and I went to graduate school. We moved into a nicer neighborhood and got a better home. I got a part-time job while in graduate school so we could have more things. We thought all our dreams were being fulfilled. We started moving up in the world, getting more of the world's goods.

As I acquired more education and greater experience in the work place, I began to discover the disparity between what men and women were paid. My frustration with the system led me to explore the feminist movement. It wasn't long before I became a very adamant feminist.

Equal pay for equal work was the cause that attracted me to feminism but I was unaware of the spirit behind the movement. It was not long before I began to resent men in general because they had oppressed women for centuries and my husband in particular because he had oppressed me. (How I wasn't exactly sure.) I was angry and resentful most of the time. Michael's way of dealing with this hostility at home was to start working 14 hours a day. That was fine with me.

So we each pursued our own interests. We had separate friends and we moved in separate circles. Each day we moved farther apart. Yet every Sunday we went to church. Everyone thought we were the model couple. Nobody would have ever known there was anything wrong, because we projected a very peaceful, happy facade. It was phony, yes, but, we didn't realize how phony. We just believed that was the way we were supposed to be. We didn't face the fact that in reality nothing was wonderful.

Love Reaches Out

For some time, my mother-in-law had been attending a Bible study and kept inviting me to go with her. My only experience with studying the Bible had been two semesters of Bible in college in which I had been taught that the Bible was a collection of simple stories written for simple-minded people. Noah's ark never existed, Adam and Eve were a myth, and Jonah was never swallowed by a whale. By the end of that course, I was convinced that the Bible was a book of fairy tales and immediately tossed the one out that I had purchased for the class.

So, when I was invited to that Bible study, all I could imagine was listening to someone read fairy tales. She kept asking me, though, for almost two years. Then one afternoon she came by our house on the way to her Bible study. I had received a very sad letter from a dear friend and I was feeling badly. She encouraged me, "Come to the Bible study and we'll pray for her." I thought, "It can't hurt."

By then, I wasn't even sure that God existed but I kept going to church just in case. I guess it was life insurance. If He did exist, I didn't want to get on His bad side. I had always feared God. I thought He was angry with me and very displeased with the way I lived.

I wasn't assured of any relationship with Him and thought surely He would reject me if it came to that. I feared death because I didn't know what it held for me. I thought if my list of good deeds was longer than my list of bad deeds on the day I died, I had a chance. If the bad things I had done outnumbered the good, hell might just be where I was heading.

That's where my heart was when I went to the Bible study that day. I thought it was just going to be one more religious experience, but I'd never met any people like those people. Twelve women sat around a dining room table and kept saying, "Hallelujah," and "Praise God," and "Look what Jesus said," and asking "You know what Jesus did for me last week?" I watched them and thought, "What do they mean what He did for you last week? He's too busy to be concerned about you."

When they read the Bible, they got so excited they just bubbled, "God said this to me." I thought, "God didn't say that to you, that was Paul. He wrote it to the Corinthians or the Romans. He wasn't talking to you!"

I was a very angry person at that time in my life and, as I said, I was an adamant feminist—very militant, very assertive. When the Bible study was over, I stood up and told them what I thought of them. I said that they were crazy if they thought that Word was alive, they were nuts—that it was written thousands of years ago and it was dead—that Jesus didn't care two hoots about what happened to them last week, and if they thought they could pray to Him and get results like that they were fooling themselves.

I loved to fight and I was ready for a good one. I just stood there with my fists clenched, ready for them to say something and then I was going to prove them wrong. No one said a word, though. They all just sat there around that table and smiled at me.

Then I knew they were crazy and I wanted one thing and one thing only—to get out of that room. One of the women looked right into my eyes and said, "You know, Marilyn, Jesus loves you." That hit me like somebody punched me in the stomach and I *knew* I had to get out of that room.

As I bolted for the door, the hostess, Claire, threw herself between me and that exit I was so desperately seeking. She later said the Lord had told her it was now or never. She just stood there with her arms out and I ran right into her. She threw her arms around me and said, "Oh! Marilyn, your heart is so troubled."

I didn't think my heart was troubled at all until she said that. Then I burst into tears. You have to understand how unusual that was for me. I didn't cry. If you ran over my foot with a steam roller, I would not cry. You wouldn't know I was hurt. I might go home and cry, but I certainly wouldn't cry in front of you. I was into power and people in power don't cry.

Yet there I was crying in front of those people and I didn't even know why. Next thing I knew they all came over and formed a circle around me and started praying. Then I *really* wanted to get out of that place. I tried, but I couldn't get out the door and everybody was praying over me. I became desperate.

Finally I found an opening and darted out the door. As I ran across the lawn, I promised myself I would never go around those people again. I decided there was definitely something wrong with them.

That evening Jan, one of the younger women from the Bible study, called me and said, "There are some people in town tonight from Chicago and I really think you'd enjoy hearing them." I didn't want to repeat any of that recent experience and so I said, "Look! I don't want to hear them. I don't want you to bother me anymore. Just leave me alone."

I think about that sometimes now, when I talk to people who say, "Get out of my life." My first reaction is to get out of their life. Thank God Jan didn't do that. She called me and invited me again the next day. I said, "Didn't you understand me last night, I told you to get out of my life and leave me alone. I don't want to hear them. I don't want any more of this Bible stuff. Just leave me alone."

She called me again the next day. She said, "Marilyn, they are still in town and I really think you might like to hear them." This time I shouted, "Don't you understand English? I don't want to go. I want you to leave me alone." I said a few other things which I won't repeat right now. I told her in no uncertain terms to get out of my life.

She called me again the next day. I realized that those women were never going to get off my back if I didn't go, so I told her, "Okay, I'll go tonight, but don't ask me again after tonight." I praise God now that she was that faithful!

An Encounter With Jesus

I was expecting a church when we arrived at somebody's house. The living room was filled with people singing and clapping and praising the Lord. The first thing that struck me was I hadn't realized there were that many of those people. Obviously they were all over the place.

When the speaker, a man named Bob Johnson, announced he was going to talk about worship, I thought, "Oh, yuk! How boring," but it was anything but that! The only thing I remember him saying that whole evening was, *worship is kissing Jesus*. I thought about that the rest of the time he spoke—kissing Jesus—that made Him a person. I thought, "This guy knows Jesus in a way that I don't."

Then he gave an altar call. I had never heard of an altar call in all of my life and I didn't have any idea what it was. He said, "There are some of you here tonight who have never asked Jesus into your heart." Then he said, "Right now, we are going to give you a chance."

Right away I thought, "Don't you dare come near me." I really thought they gave you a card or something when you accepted Jesus, and they were going to come around and check. I just sat there with my fists clenched, glued to that chair, and thought, "If they ask me, I'm going to tell them a thing or two." Of course, nobody asked me.

People began standing up all around me and I wondered what was going on. When a young girl stood up behind me, several people rushed forward and exclaimed, "We've been praying for you for eight years." I turned around and looked into her tear-stained face wondering what on earth someone could have done to need prayers for eight years. Very shortly the room was filled with laughter and rejoicing. I wasn't sure what had happened, but I sensed it must have been something wonderful.

The people I came with didn't want to leave right away, so I had to stand around afterwards and listen while they all ate snacks and drank coffee. I really just wanted to get out of there, but I started listening to them and, again, they were talking like Jesus walked with them every day of the week. He did this, He did that, He was with me, the Holy Spirit told me this. And I started wondering. "How did they get this? What did they do to get a relationship like that?

The next night they called me, again. They said, "This is their last night in town, do you want to go?" I thought, "Well, it wouldn't hurt," so I went. This time the meeting was in a church. It wasn't one of those "home meetings" that I thought were subversive. God meets us right where we are.

As we climbed the stairs to the meeting place, people behind me were exclaiming, "It's in an upper room, of all places!" I failed to see the significance of that and thought once again that these people were all a little bit crazy.

When I came in, people were clapping their hands and singing. It was extremely hard for me to clap my hands. When you came from a background of quiet prayer it is really hard to make noise in church. It was as if I had arthritis. I simply could not get my hands to come together. So I just sat there as everybody around me shouted and praised God.

This time I wasn't resentful. I just wanted to hear what the speaker had to say. He began to talk about the fact that Jesus died for *me*. All my life when I thought of Jesus hanging on the cross, I had been one in a crowd of millions. I didn't even know if He knew I was in the crowd, I was just out there. I also prided myself in never having committed adultery or murdered anyone, so I really didn't think I personally needed a Savior. I had always been glad that Jesus died for all those other poor, unfortunate sinners, though, because I had benefited from their gain.

As the speaker talked that night, all of a sudden I knew Jesus died for *me*. Suddenly I realized what a wretched sinner I was. It was not the sins that I had committed or not committed, it was that my very nature was that of a sinner. I was standing at the foot of the Cross and Jesus was dying for *me*. I never knew He even cared for me! I was just in awe that He loved me that much and that He died for me. I felt His wondrous love pouring out to me and I knew I was precious. I couldn't wait for that altar call. I didn't even know what they called it, but I thought, "Oh! I hope they do that thing that they did last night." And, of course, they did.

Then as I started to jump to my feet and go forward, there was another part of me that said, "You don't need to do this. We already have it. You're in the one true church that is heaven bound. They're the ones that need to do this but you got it. You don't have to stand up and go forward. Don't make a fool of yourself." A battle raged within me. My heart was aching to go but it was like I had lead in my shoes and something fought to keep me seated.

Finally I just jumped up and the minute I got out in the aisle, the battle was over. When I took that step of obedience, the Lord was right there to meet me. I was born again that night and the entire course of my life changed.

A House Divided

When I went home that night I was bubbling over. I exclaimed to Michael, "I found Jesus!" He looked at me and asked, "When was He lost?" I tried again, "I've been saved!" "From what," he asked. Finally in frustration I exclaimed, "I found the Lord, I'm born again." He looked at me like I had two heads. "Well, good!" was his only reply. He'd already been through phase after phase in my life and he thought this was just another one. As hard as it was for him to understand what had happened in my life, there was more to come.

I became a faithful attendee at the Bible study. Just a few weeks later the women informed me that I needed the Baptism of the Holy Spirit. I had never heard of that so I asked them to explain it to me. They explained and I said, "That's okay, I've got Jesus, I don't need that." They persisted, "You don't understand. It's not an option. It comes next." I said, "I'm fine where I am."

The next week, they greeted me with, "Are you ready to receive the Baptism?" By then I had realized that those people never gave up so I gave in, "Okay, pray over me, but I don't want those tongues that you got. I'm making that clear, right now. I'm not getting them, and that's that."

They were undaunted. I could see I was getting nowhere fast so I said, "Maybe for you it came with the package, but I don't want them. I don't need them."

They prayed over me and told me I could now speak in a new language. I was very indignant, "I told you, I don't want tongues. I'm not going to take them and that's that. I want everything else that comes with the Baptism. I want the power, and everything else, but not the tongues."

I continued believing that way for probably a good six weeks. Then one evening I attended my first healing service. Charles and Frances Hunter were ministering and I saw one miracle after another. I had never seen anything like that in my life yet I was very skeptical that any of what I was seeing was real. I was convinced they hired those people to say publicly that they were healed.

Since then Charles and Frances have become dear friends of ours and I know how completely sincere they are. I's hard to believe I was so sceptical back then, but I was. As I watched people falling under the power of the Holy Spirit that night, I just knew that it was all fake. I was about to tell my dear friend, Jan, who had brought me that evening, what I thought of all of it, when she hit the deck, clanging into a metal chair on the cement floor. I knew Jan and I trusted her. She had led me to Jesus. Surely if she fell under the power of God, it had to be real. I suddenly had new eyes of faith.

At the end of the service Charles and Frances said, "Let's just praise God for all that He has done tonight." We all raised our hands and everyone began praising and singing to Him in tongues. I was doing the best I could in English when all of a sudden I knew I had something else to say to Him. Something inside of me wanted to come out, and I didn't know how to say it. English just seemed inadequate.

I kept saying, "Oh, I love You, Lord, I love You, I love You!" All these wonderfully strange words were swirling about within me but Satan fights so hard against the Baptism. He was saying, "You've heard Latin all your life. You used to pray in Latin at church. That's what you're hearing. That's not tongues, that's Latin."

I believed those thoughts so I kept praising the Lord in English. Finally, though, I couldn't stand it any more and I said, "I don't care if it is Latin or not, I want to say it to the Lord." I said a couple of words and my prayer language began tumbling out. I realized I'd had it all that time, from the time they first prayed over me, and it was my own stubborn head that kept me from receiving it.

An incredibly wonderful thing began happening in my life after that. The Word was more alive to me, old fears I had battled for years disappeared when I prayed in tongues, I was bolder in sharing Jesus with others.

I became like a sponge. I went to every prayer meeting, every Bible study, attended every ministry meeting that came into town. I didn't know anything about my home being my first place to minister. I was gone seven days a week absorbing, absorbing, absorbing the Word.

Michael really began to resent what I was doing. Before I had been into work and into the world and didn't pay any attention to him and now I was into the Lord and didn't pay any attention to him. I made a lot of mistakes. I practically beat him over the head with my Bible. "You've got to get saved and read this Word. What's wrong with you? Shape up." What I thought but didn't say was perhaps worse than what I did. "God isn't as pleased with you as He is with me" was the underlying message in all that I shared with him. I wanted so badly for Michael to have what I had, but I didn't know how to go about it. I really made a mess of things.

A Return to the World

Six months after I accepted Jesus we built a home in the mountains and moved there. Michael loved the mountains and he wanted to live there. I loved the city and I didn't want to move, so I became resentful and angry. I stalked up there with him and plunked down our furniture, but in my heart I was still in the city.

Very shortly I discovered another drawback to living in the mountains. I missed the teachings I'd gone to in Denver. It all stopped when we moved to the mountains and I felt like I was in the desert. I kept asking, "God! Where are You? What happened to You? Where'd You go?" All those Christians I thought were everywhere didn't seem to be in Evergreen. At least, I couldn't find them.

In the first six months of my walk with the Lord I had grown to believe that everybody who called themselves Christians were born again and baptized in the Holy Spirit. So in my search for Christians in the mountains, I asked everyone I met if they were a Christian. When someone said yes, I'd say, "Oh! Hallelujah!" and throw my arms around them. They'd quickly back away and look at me strangely. I couldn't figure out what was wrong.

After I'd alienated about three quarters of Evergreen, I finally discovered that something was different about the people who called themselves Christians and those fanatics I had grown to love in Denver. Finally I asked the Lord to lead me to some of those fanatics. I figured there had to be some somewhere in those hills.

Soon I joined a little Bible study in a very dry church. I don't know how many times I attended, perhaps two or three, but I am sure it was just so I could meet a wonderful sister in the Lord named Jackie. During one of the lengthy discussions of scriptural validity, she very quietly but very firmly stated, "I believe Jesus still heals today."

I was astounded! Maybe she was a Christian like those I had known in Denver. A few days later I saw her in the grocery store and timidly approached her. (By then I had learned not to rush people.) "Are you one of us?" I whispered next to the canned vegetables. She smiled and said, "I sure am!" At last I had found a friend in the Lord! I latched onto her and in the ensuing weeks found out there were quite a few of those "fanatics" in those hills.

Very shortly after I started to get back on track spiritually, I got a call from a hospital in Denver. They had an administrative position open in Out Patient Nursing. Satan really dangled a carrot in front of me and I jumped for it. It sounded so good. It was a high-powered position, required a good deal of expertise and promised to be a challenge. Not only would it give me the opportunity to further my career, but I took the job with the idea that I was going to save the world. I was crusading for Jesus. I was going to go to that hospital and save everybody in that clinic. Maybe even everyone in the hospital.

One little thing I didn't realize, though. You can't change the world unless your Jerusalem is in order and my Jerusalem was a mess. Michael and I didn't even know each other anymore. We just drifted in and out of the same house. I didn't know anything about a wife's scriptural role.

Instead of me transforming the world, the world transformed me. I began to backslide. I couldn't find time to read the Word consistently. Pray became a cry in crisis only. I started smoking again. My language slipped back into what it was before I knew Jesus. The old feminist anger rose up once again in me. My relationship with the Lord began to disintegrate.

Since the birth of Mike, Jr., I had really wanted another baby. During my days of working in the hospital I had two very emotionally painful miscarriages and ultimately having another child became an obsession with me. Michael didn't want another child and had actually rejoiced at the loss of the two babies. That made me even more angry and resentful.

He was working evenings then and I was working days. I was exhausted when I came home from work so I handled things on a crisis basis. Whatever was the first crisis got attention. Then the second crisis got attention. It was usually children, dinner, laundry in that order.

By the time Mike got off work, I didn't have any energy or any time for him. Usually I was asleep when he came home, so we really had absolutely no relationship at that point. It was worse than it had ever been. I threw all my hopes and dreams into the baby that I wanted, the one I could love and could love me back. I was convinced that Jesus wanted to give me that baby.

About March of that year, God began to show me

that I was getting into serious trouble. There were men at work in whom I was becoming very interested. They showed me affection that Michael did not. They showed an interest in me that he did not and I was very close to getting sexually involved with one of them.

The Lord told me, "It is time for you to go home." I really didn't have any purpose or direction. I was just running. Many people tried to undermine what God was doing. They asked me. "What are you going to do at home? You have talent, you have knowledge and they are going to be wasted in the home."

One doctor that I'd thought was a Christian asked me, "Why are you going home?" and I said, "I believe the Lord wants to teach me about being a wife and a mother." He started laughing and said, "Do you really believe all that Paulist garbage? Paul was just a chauvinist." In my heart I was beginning to believe that.

So that's how I left work and returned home. There wasn't any joy in my heart. I was just getting out of the fire.

The days dragged on. I wandered around the house, trying to find purpose for my life. I didn't know anything about caring for my family or organizing our home. When I worked, I had grown used to doing everything in five-minute intervals. After work each day, I'd throw laundry in while I cooked dinner. Now, all of a sudden, I had day after day in which to do laundry, cook meals, vacuum rugs. I had no daily goals, no periodic job performance interviews, no rewards for good performance. There were no committee meetings for strategic planning. I just didn't know what to do.

The Other Woman

If Satan can't sidetrack you one way, he tries another. In my desire to become a perfect Christian wife, I began taking classes. In some rather strange classes, I learned that a submissive wife is one that makes no decisions whatsoever. Her husband decides everything. It seemed very foreign to me, but then everything in my life had changed since I received Jesus. So, I just turned off my brain and began asking Michael if I should do the laundry or go to the grocery store.

Poor Michael didn't know what to do with me. He said , "I married a bright girl but this Christianity has turned you into a vegetable. What's wrong with you?" I became angry and thought, "Here I am trying to be submissive and you don't even care, so I'll just go back to my old ways." Yet I knew that wasn't what the Lord wanted, so I would try once again to be submissive by their definition. Praise God! He had His hand on us even though my bouncing from one extreme to another wasn't bringing much stability to our relationship.

During the following summer, God began dealing with me about my overwhelming desire to have a baby. The scripture He used was 1 Samuel 1:8. Hannah, who was Samuel's mother, was obsessed with having a baby. Every year she would cry out to God for a child. Her husband Elkanah said to her, "Am I not worth more to you than ten sons?"

The Lord really dealt with me, "I've given you a husband and you aren't even ministering to him. You just see him as a means of getting a child." I thought about that and realized I had been doing just that. Then the Lord asked me, "Can you give up your desire for a baby to Me."

It wasn't an easy thing. I knew full well what He was asking and I mourned that baby as if it had died. I went through two weeks of crying, of laying down my desire for another child and then taking it back, and laying it down and taking it back, laying it down and taking it back. Finally, one day I laid down that desire and walked away from it. I had cried it through and settled it.

Then I asked the Lord to teach me to be the wife He wanted me to be. During the next few months He began teaching me to love and honor my husband. All my concentration was turned toward Michael and then, when I least expected it, I got pregnant. I truly had given up that child and never expected to have another baby and now God was blessing me with one.

As much of a shock as it was to me, Michael felt I had planned the whole thing. He thought I had lied to him saying I was giving up the desire to have a child but secretly planned to get pregnant. He said, "You just use your Christianity to manipulate things. You lied to me."

It was the straw that broke the camels back. Michael just shut me off. When I look back, we were so far apart we didn't know how to talk to each other anymore. We didn't even realize how great the problem was until our avalanche started. Then it was as if everything we had ever known began tumbling downhill.

During that time we were close friends with a couple at church. We had dinner with them a lot, went out with them often, and just spent a lot of time together. She was my best friend. She began inviting me over for coffee and said things to me like, " Things must be really tough. You're pregnant and Michael doesn't want the baby." I was eager to talk about how terrible things were and I poured out my heart to her.

Unfortunately I didn't know the scripture, "She does her husband good and never evil all the days of her life." Instead I dumped garbage about my husband at my friend's doorstep. I didn't know it but she wanted my husband. She took everything I gave her and turned it around to bless him. She told him, "You poor man! Your wife's pregnant and that must be really tough. You don't want the baby and she doesn't understand you." She was holding the gun that would nearly destroy our marriage, but I gave her all the ammunition she needed.

The Holy Spirit was warning me very clearly about their relationship, but I kept making excuses. I thought, "She's such a good friend. She's such a nice person. I'm judging her. That's not fair." I ignored all the warnings God gave me.

Every time I would become suspicious, she'd have me over for coffee, or we'd get invited for dinner and I would think, "Well, there couldn't be anything wrong if they're having us over. That would be stupid."

She began calling Michael over to her house to help her. Her husband worked long hours, and so she'd call Michael at all hours of the day and night. She needed help with things that didn't work, or were stopped up, and so he'd go over to help her. I really resented it because there were a bunch of things around our house that didn't work and *they* weren't getting fixed.

I remembered once hearing a teaching that men liked doing things for others because they don't get praised enough when they do them at home. So I started going into a big gala of praise every time Michael would do something, even the smallest of things. It was really phony, though, because my only motivation was to get him to stay home.

Michael continued to reject me and the coming baby, but all along the way the Lord gave me encouragement, "I have My hand on you and this baby is in My timing."

Just before our baby was born I went to talk with my best friend. I still didn't suspect anything serious, but I went to her as a friend and I asked her to please stop calling my husband because I needed him. I needed him home not over at her house fixing her plumbing and taking out her garbage and whatever else she needed.

A few days later, we were at a party at her house and I overheard a conversation between Michael and her and it was very obvious that the two of them were making plans to go off together. I just fell apart. I left the party and got into my car. I drove and I drove. I remember it was raining and I was crying so hard I could hardly see the road. I didn't want to go home, but I didn't know where I wanted to go. I really wanted to die. I even thought about driving the car off the road and just killing myself. I kept thinking, "Lord, You can take me home right now."

He didn't, though, and eventually I had to go back to our house.

A Quality Decision

Michael was home by the time I got there. I begged him to stop seeing her. I pleaded, "Stop this relationship now, I need you. The baby needs you." He answered, "Forget it, I don't need you, I don't want you, I don't love you."

I've never in my life fallen apart like I did that night. I honestly could feel my body falling in pieces all over and I couldn't pick them up again. I began weeping and I became hysterical. I sat on the edge of the bathtub in the dark and rocked back and forth and cried for hours. I was afraid to move because I felt that if I did, I would disintegrate, just fall into a hundred thousand pieces.

All that time Michael sat in the next room and listened but he never once came to talk to me. Perhaps that hurt worse than knowing he wanted her more than he wanted me. Finally, when I pulled myself together, he said, "You really need counseling. You're never going to be able to make it through this divorce if you don't get some counseling." I knew he was right.

So Michael agreed to go to counseling to ensure that I got there, but he wanted to pick the counselor. I wanted a Christian, of course, but he said, "No way." He picked a man that we had known from previous years who was a very good secular counselor, but was undoubtedly an atheist. I was afraid to go to such an ungodly man for counsel, but a friend of mine prayed with me. She said, "We're going to agree that God is going to use this counselor. God's going to speak through him even though he doesn't know he's being used." God honored that prayer because that was one of the things that did happen—eventually.

At first, though, things looked very bleak. After our first session with him, the counselor said, "There's nothing I can do for this marriage. You are hundreds of miles apart. You no longer have any interest in each other. There's no way we can paste this back together. Get a quick divorce and save yourselves time and money." Of course, that is just what Michael wanted to hear. He said, "See, now we've gone for counseling and it didn't work."

In the midst of all this, the full impact of Michael's adulterous relationship finally hit me. Perhaps the Lord had protected me or I'd just been naive until then. I don't know which it was but I hadn't realized how deeply involved they were. When the full impact of it finally hit me, I didn't know what to do. I wondered if there was someone, somewhere who could help us.

I went to our pastor on Sunday morning and shared the whole situation with him. Michael's new love and her husband were also in our church and I fully expected our pastor to take a stand against the relationship. Instead, he explained to me that when a marriage is over, it is over. He said that if Michael didn't want to reconcile there was nothing I could do to change the situation.

In one last attempt to find someone who would help me, I called on a friend of ours who was a born again, Spirit-filled pastor. I knew that he knew the Word and could tell me what scripture had to say about all this. After I explained the situation to him, he said, "According to Matthew 19 you have scriptural grounds for divorce. Since Michael has been in adultery, God releases you from this marriage and will bring you another husband." After that conversation I went home to prepare for divorce.

When we make Jesus Lord of our lives, though, He has the right to speak to our hearts and overrule the counsel of men. That afternoon Jesus did just that. He took me to 1 Corinthians 7:10 and 11, *Now to the married I give this command, yet not I but the Lord: A wife is not to depart from her husband. But even if she does depart, let her remain unmarried or be reconciled to her husband. And a husband is not to divorce his wife.*

The Lord made it clear to me that those were my two options. If I chose to remain single, He promised me He would be my husband and a father to my children." If I chose to reconcile, He promised He would teach me how. I knew that either choice would be a blessing to me. I knew that if I honored God's choices, He would keep His Word to me. I had to make the decision.

I was pregnant with our third child and I really wanted him to know his father. I wanted our other two children to grow up knowing their father. I wanted my marriage healed if it were at all possible, but I couldn't imagine how.

Finally I chose to reconcile, but I was honest with the Lord, "I don't even know how to start, Lord." His answer blessed me, "That's okay, I do."

The Lord began my training. It seemed to me the logical place to begin was with Michael's problems but the Lord began by dealing with my heart. He said, "I can't begin to do anything with this situation until you forgive." Well, I didn't want to forgive because I had been hurt and rejected. With every ounce of energy I had I was trying to hold things together and now God was telling me, "You've got to forgive. I can't do another thing until you forgive."

So I wrestled with forgiving Michael first. You know it's not too hard to forgive someone you love even though they've hurt you a lot. You can even forgive them over and over and over again. So, forgiving my husband came within a few hours after God spoke to my heart. Forgiving the other woman proved to be another matter, though.

Eyes of Faith

She had used my friendship. She had betrayed me. She had lied to me. She had done a lot of things. She had given up all pretense of friendship once things were out in the open and I didn't want to forgive her. I hated her. I just wanted to see her rot in hell and I didn't care what God did with her. I wanted Him to strike her down with lightning and get rid of her. God said, "You can't do that. It won't work. You must forgive her. You must learn to love her."

I walked around the house for eight hours trying to get away from the Lord. I cried out, "It's not fair, God. I don't want to forgive her. Just leave me alone." I'd try to get away from Him but He'd be right there with me. He'd say, "Are you ready?" and I'd say, "No!" and would walk into another room.

Finally I got in my car. Somehow I thought God wasn't going to get in the car with me. He did, though. I didn't see Him sitting there, but I knew His presence was there. I knew He was waiting for me to forgive her.

So, I went to a friend's house to tell her what had happened. I really expected her to be sympathetic to my cause. Instead the first words out of her mouth were, "You've got to forgive her. Have you done it?"

I didn't want to hear that. I got back into the car and started driving. I continued to argue with God, "You don't understand what I've been through," I said. "You don't know what it is like to be betrayed by a friend." And the Lord said, "Don't I?"

All of a sudden, I had a new understanding of what happened in the Garden of Gethsemane. Jesus wasn't in turmoil just because He knew He had to be tortured and die. All of a sudden, I had a new understanding of what happened when Judas, who was a friend, betrayed Him with a kiss, an expression of love. Jesus knew the pain of betrayal. He knew the pain of abandonment, too. The disciples He loved couldn't even stay awake one hour with Him. They went off and did their own thing.

So I then took the tactic that she didn't want to be forgiven. She didn't care that she had sinned. She probably didn't even recognize it as sin, and that I didn't have to forgive her if she didn't want to be forgiven.

Then the Lord reminded me about the Cross and His words, *Father forgive them.* He said, "They didn't want to be forgiven, either. They thought they were doing something good. It doesn't matter if she doesn't want to be forgiven, you've got to forgive her."

I continued to try every argument I could think of until finally I was exhausted. I gave in, "All right, I'll do it, but all I can do is *will* to forgive her. My emotions say I hate her, but Your Word says that I have to forgive her and that You'll only forgive me as I forgive her. So, I will to forgive her, Lord, and that is all I can do." He said, "That's enough."

I was so scared. "Now what do I do? It's hopeless. I can see the hundreds of mistakes I made through the years. I know I made them and I repent of them, but what do I do now? I can't paste it all back together, and Michael won't even talk to me."

It was then that God began to teach me through words that friends gave me and through what He spoke to my heart. He said, "What does My Word say about your marriage?" So I began to search the scriptures for things that God said about marriage. I began to write them down in a little notebook. Every time He gave me a scripture, I would write it down and personalize it. I'd put Michael's name in it, or I'd put my name in it, or the children's. I began claiming those scriptures and believing them for us.

Then the Lord spoke to my heart again and said, "You have to have a faith vision of what your marriage is going to be like when it is healed, and what your husband is going to be like when he is healed." So I asked the Lord for *His* vision for Michael and He took me to I Timothy 3:2-7.

I was amazed by the Lord. I just wanted Michael to come home. I wanted him to love me and to want our children. The Word God gave me for him, though, described an elder. God had much bigger plans for Michael. I felt like Sarah in the tent. I laughed at the impossibility of what God was saying.

God began to show me how I had prayed for my husband for years, "Lord, just let him be saved. Just let him be saved. Just let him be saved." God said, "Are you going to pray that same way again? Or are you going to pray My will for that man?" I took a good look at that scripture and from that day on, I started praying God's way. I put Michael's name in there and prayed that *Michael is above reproach, the husband of but one wife, temperate, self-controlled, respectable, hospitable, able to teach, not given to much wine, not violent but gentle, not quarrel-*

some, not a lover of money. He manages his own family well and sees that his children obey him with proper respect. I wrote it in my notebook and I started claiming it every day. I said, "That's Michael. That's who God wants Michael to be."

Every time Michael came home he would say things like, "I don't love you, and I don't want to be around you. I really wish you'd get out of my life and I wish you'd take these kids. I don't want them." Satan uses the mouths of loved ones when we are in a spiritual battle. They say things to us that really cut, but we've got to recognize that our loved ones are not the enemy. Satan is our real enemy. I had to realize that my husband was saying things to me that reflected how my true enemy felt about me. He was just the messenger. So when Michael came home and said those terrible things, I'd read the scripture again and realize that God's plan for him was much greater than Satan's.

You must also recognize that you are in a spiritual battle and you've got to fight for your marriage on a spiritual level. You too must realize that your spouse is not your enemy. Once you begin fighting for your marriage with spiritual weapons, you have the advantage over the enemy. He knows that and is going to work very hard to keep your eyes on the circumstances.

Words of Life

I'll share some of the scriptures with you that God gave me, but ask the Lord for ones tailor-made for you. He is going to give you scriptures and words of prophecy that will speak to you right where you are now.

One of my biggest concerns was our children. By this time our third child, Jason, had been born. Now I had three little ones to protect. With all the confusion, all the turmoil, and all the anger that was going on around them, I asked the Lord for a word for them. He gave me Isaiah 54:13, *All your sons will be taught by the Lord and great will be the peace of your children.* I put our children's names in there. I said, "All of my children will be taught of the Lord and great will be the peace of Cristine, and great will be the peace of Mike, and great will be the peace of Jason."

There's a scripture in Jeremiah 32:39 that says, *I will give them singleness of heart and action so that they will always fear me for their own good and for the good of their children after them.* I put our names in there. I said, "I will give Marilyn and Michael singleness of heart and action so they will always fear me for their own good and for the good of Cristine, Mike, and Jason." I began to stand on those scriptures, and I began to believe and to pray them as things got worse, darker, and uglier.

Michael came home one day and said, "I'm getting a divorce and there is nothing else that can be done. I don't want you. I never did. I'm going to marry her." Things looked very bleak.

One of the scriptures I had been praying was in Psalm 35. It said, *May your enemies be as chaff before the wind.* I prayed that for her. I said, "Lord, may she be as chaff before the wind. May You blow her to some other place. Get her out of this picture, so we can not have this problem." God was gracious. He took her out of the picture. Michael discovered that divorcing me was going to cost him a great deal of money the way the courts were going to split our assets, so he sent her away, back to her husband in another state. At least one family had been reunited.

That didn't solve our problem, though, because the problem was not her. She was just an instrument Satan had used. The problem was us. So after she was gone my husband said, " I know she's not what I wanted, but I don't want you either. I want a divorce. I want to be single again. I want to date and have a good time."

Another Scripture that I had been claiming was Proverbs 5 and 7, the warnings against adultery and the adulterous woman. I put Michael's name in there and I claimed that every day.

Michael was going to single's bars again, double dating with friends of ours who were cheating on their wives. Every single one of those couples are now divorced. I know it is the Word of God that was mighty in our situation that took us to victory over the enemy.

Circumstances kept getting darker and darker. I thought, "God, I'm praying Your Word, I'm standing, and I'm believing. What's wrong? Why doesn't it seem to be working?"

Then one day the Lord took me to Genesis. At the very beginning it says, "And God *said* let there be light and there was light, and God *said* this and there was this, and God *said* that and there was that." He showed me that when Satan came to tempt Jesus, Jesus *said* to him, "It is written." He *said* it to him. He didn't sit there and think, "It is written." He *said* it.

I began to see that all through scripture when the situation changed it was because God spoke or His Word was spoken. I realized I hadn't been doing that. I had just been sitting there every day quietly claiming those words but I had to speak them. Jason was little then and I'd walk through the house with him and speak the words that God gave me. I'd speak them into the air-ways of the house and I'd command the situation to come in line with God's Word. I'd command our marriage to come in line with what God said about it.

Whenever Michael came home and continued to say whatever Satan used him to say, I'd just "house clean" again the minute he left. I'd go through the house and speak what God said.

I wish I could tell you that I was perfect in doing this. I wish I could tell you that I was never angry, never bitter, never upset. I wasn't perfect. I had a lot of hard times and a lot of days in which I was so angry with Michael I didn't even want him anymore. I didn't care what God did with him. He could have dropped him off the face of the earth and that would have been fine with me, but God showed me that I couldn't afford those emotions.

Satan comes with self pity and tells us how much

we have suffered. He'll send people to you all the time to tell you they don't know how you do it, you have endured so much. The minute you open that door to self pity, though, Satan kicks it open a little farther and gets in there with anger. Soon you're incredibly mad at your spouse. You're ready to kill because of what you have endured. If Satan can get the door open that far, he kicks it open farther. Then you develop bitterness and it starts taking root. Scripture tells us that a root of bitterness defiles many (Hebrews 12:15). A bitter person is like poison. No one wants to be around them.

The Lord made it clear that self pity is not something we can afford to entertain for even a minute. After I finally learned that lesson I refused to listen to people trying to help me feel sorry for myself.

Within two weeks of the time that I started confessing God's Word out loud, Michael came home. I praise God that he taught me that lesson, and He taught it to me fast. It really helped me to weather the storms that were yet to come.

Order Brings Healing

When Michael came home, it was not at all how I had pictured it. He said, "I'm only here for a little while. I'm trying to get my head together. Don't expect me to love you. Don't expect me to care for you. I'm on my way out. I'm just taking a little breather here." At that time he began building a house for himself.

I went to God and asked, "This is what I prayed for? You sent me home this guy that says he doesn't want me and he's going to move. It doesn't seem to be any better than before. Now what do I do?"

I realized then that my own love for Michael was dead. I had no emotions left for him. I had fought so long and so hard, and stood, and believed, and suddenly he was there and I didn't know what to do with him. I just didn't want him around anymore. I thought, "Why did I even bother?" I went to the Lord again and asked, "What do I do now? Even if you give him back to me, I don't know if I want him, Lord."

The Lord took me to Genesis 3, where He spoke to Eve. The line He took me to was, "Your desire will be for your husband..." The Lord had me read it again and again until I understood what He was saying.

I was still thinking of Eve. Of course, her desire would be for her husband. She didn't have a whole lot of options. It wasn't as if she could go out and get George or somebody. All she had was Adam.

The Lord continued to minister to me. All of a sudden, I had a new understanding of Eve and what she experienced. If there ever was a woman that could say to her husband, "Boy! Did you blow it," it was Eve. Her husband not only ruined it for them, but he ruined it for the whole human race. They were living in luxury in that beautiful garden and they had everything they needed when suddenly they were kicked out. She had to go through pain in childbirth, the ground was cursed, and her husband had to work by the sweat of his brow.

I began to understand what Eve was feeling. She could have become so hard-hearted, so hateful of her man and said, "Nothing will ever be the same again." She would have been right, nothing has ever been the same since.

God began to speak to me, "I am talking to you, right there, not to Eve, that your desire will be for your husband." He began to show me that I had to set my will with God's will. I had to will that my desire would be for my husband because there was no desire there anymore. I struggled with that for awhile and finally said, "Okay, Lord. My desire will be for my husband. I will it. You work out the details."

As God began to change my heart toward my husband, He also began to deal with me about the spiritual headship of our home. For so long I had held things together, both naturally and spiritually. I had always felt that I would continue in that role until Michael grew in the Lord and was ready to take over. Now God began dealing with me that headship was an assigned position, not an earned one. It was not up to me to vote for Michael when I thought he was ready. The Lord had made him head of our home the day we got married.

This was a real shock to me. I knew that Michael was rejecting the things of God. He didn't read the Bible or seek the Lord for direction. The whole idea of him leading our family was one of the most frightening concepts I had ever heard. I refused to accept it.

Again, God just followed me around and said, "You can't do anything until you listen to Me and you do what I ask you to do." I cried and argued with God. I said, "You don't know what You're asking. How come he gets to be in charge when he messed up everything? I really feel that I am better qualified for the position of being in charge here."

God began to deal with me. "I don't care what you think you're qualified for, the position of headship is not in vacancy. There's no option. You don't qualify for it in My sight, and the only way I'm going to be able to heal this marriage is for you to understand that your husband is the head of this household, that he is the spiritual head. He's in charge here and you need to submit to him and honor him as unto Me." I replied, "Lord, You don't know what You are asking."

Then He led me to the Amplified Bible to what it says concerning submission. *Let the wife see that she respects and reverences her husband. That she notices him, regards him, honors him, prefers him, venerates and esteems him. That she defers to him praises him, loves and admires him exceedingly.* God said to me, "That's what I am asking of you, right now."

I thought, "Oh! Lord, How can you ask this of me?" There were days of arguing with God over that one. I thought His plan had major problems, but then I saw something. Often in scripture where there is a command to the woman and a command to the man, the command to the woman comes first. Submit to your husband first and then husbands loves your wives. The Lord began to show me that sometimes that is the only way He can get through to a man. I wanted Him to get through to Michael so I started doing what He asked.

I started going to Michael and asking his advice about decisions I needed to make. These were not like the dumb questions I had asked when I first went through the weird submission teaching. These were questions regarding spiritual matters that he really needed to make a decision about. Michael wasn't very happy about this new approach and would say, "Get off my back. Leave me alone." Then I'd go back to God, "He didn't want the headship, Lord, so I took it back." And He'd say, "You can't take it back. It's not yours to take back."

Later Michael told me that God really started dealing with him when I gave up the position of headship. When he had to respond to God, when he had to deal with the awesome responsibility God had given him, he became overwhelmed. He didn't know what to do and he had to turn to God for help.

Another lie that Satan had been telling Michael was that he could never be forgiven. Adultery had always been unforgivable in Michael's book. When he crossed that line, he thought God would not forgive him. Even as the Lord was drawing Michael to Him, Michael was afraid to reach out to God because he thought He would be rejected.

About that time we were invited to a healing service. Every healing service that I'd ever been to in my life was very lively, but that evening we went into a church packed with people sitting absolutely quietly. A short, little man stood up and almost whispered, "We're going to have a healing service tonight and God is going to heal."

Then he walked up and down the aisle praying over people. He was so low key that we almost fell asleep waiting for him to get back up the isle again. I thought, "This is the dumbest thing. I don't know why on earth we're even here."

At the end of that service, he asked, "How many of you here were touched by God tonight?" Hands went up all over the church. A woman got up out of a wheel chair and began laboriously walking up the isle. But the greatest miracle of all for me was that Michael raised his hand. I just couldn't believe it. I thought, "How did you stay awake long enough for Him to talk to you?"

God showed me that night that He can use anyone and anything. He meets us where we are, and my husband wasn't ready to jump up and down. He needed a quiet moment in which the Lord could speak to him.

That night, God showed Michael that He loved him and that He had forgiven him. Michael was born again.

In February 1980 we were both baptized. It was a final step of obedience for Michael. He had told me, "You can go. I'll go with you, but I'm not going to get baptized." When we got to the water, though, Michael said, "You know, I've fought God for years. Every time He said do something. I said *no* and I held my breath and I fought. For once I'm going to say *yes*."

As Michael came up out of the waters of baptism, he began speaking in tongues. He had been baptized in the Holy Spirit. His chains were broken and he had been set free. That day Michael gave God the freedom to mold him as the man He wanted him to be.

Only One Way

From that day on we began working together to heal our marriage. It didn't happen overnight. It takes a season to build trust again, a season to build love—but that is another book.

I had to run to keep up with Michael. We joined a solid Word-based church and the Lord spent the next two years replacing the doctrine of man with the truth of His Word. Then He called us into full-time marriage ministry. We who had no hope have now been privileged to help bring hope to thousands of couples around the world! What a wonderful God we serve!

I want you to know that God is no respecter of persons. I didn't do anything special. I am not any different from you. Believe me, I made a lot of mistakes and messed up a lot of things. It just amazes me that God is so faithful. It is His perfection that brings us to victory. It has nothing to do with our own perfection. Our responsibility is to be obedient and repent when we fail to obey. He loves us so much that He wants to see us succeed more than we even do ourselves.

Our marriage was not singled out for God's blessing. He wants the same for you. Whatever the problem is with your marriage or any relationship you want to have healed, God is just as much for you as He is for us.

Satan will lie to you and tell you that our situation was a fluke—that it was a one time thing and it doesn't happen for everyone. However, it does when God's people are faithful and believe and speak His Word into situations.

You need to know that if you are fighting a battle like this, you've *got* to do it with Jesus. If you don't have a relationship with Jesus and you are trying to fight a battle in your home, you are powerless. You can't do it without Jesus. You have nothing to stand on. You must be born again.

Secondly, if you are trying to fight this battle and you are born again but not baptized in the Holy Spirit, then you are in the Army but you haven't been issued your ammunition yet. You cannot fight the battle without the power of the Holy Spirit. You need the guidance of the Holy Spirit to tell you what to pray for and to tell you how to pray at the times when you don't know how to pray. You need your prayer language to pray the perfect will of the Father into that situation.

If you desire to receive Jesus right now, it is very easy to do. You do not have to clean yourself up or straighten up your life first. That is why you need a Savior in the first place. You cannot straighten up your own life. You cannot clean yourself up to meet Jesus. You must come to Him just as you are. He will change your heart. He will clean up your life from the inside out.

Romans 10:9 and 10 say, *If you confess with your mouth the Lord Jesus and believe in your heart that God has raised Him from the dead, you will be saved. For with the heart one believes to righteousness, and with the mouth confession is made to salvation.* It's that simple. You must believe in your heart and confess Jesus as Lord and

Savior with your mouth. When you are obedient to do your part, the Lord is faithful to do His. If that is the desire of your heart, pray this prayer.

Jesus, I confess that I am a sinner and that I am powerless to change my own heart. I believe that You are Lord and that You died for my sins and were resurrected from the dead. I ask You now to forgive my sins. I turn my life over to You. I declare that You are my Lord and My Savior. I love You, Jesus, and I surrender my life to You.

If you have prayed this prayer from your heart, you are now born again. You have a new nature in Christ. God Himself lives within you now. All the promises of the Bible are now yours, but there's more!

Before Jesus ascended to Heaven after His resurrection from the dead, He told His followers to wait in Jerusalem for the Holy Spirit to come upon them. Acts 1:8 says, *But you shall receive power when the Holy Spirit has come upon you; and you shall be witnesses to Me in Jerusalem, and in all Judea, and Samaria, and to the ends of the earth.*

You need that power that Jesus was speaking of. You need the ability to pray the perfect will of God (Romans 8:26) and to pray in the Spirit when your mind is not sure what to do (1 Corinthians 14:14). If you have received Jesus as your Lord and Savior, the Baptism of the Holy Spirit is available to you today. You need only ask for it.

Jesus, I confess that You are my Lord and my Savior. I renounce all works of the enemy in my life and I ask

You to baptize me in the Holy Spirit. I desire the spiritual power that You promised. I desire to speak in other tongues that the Holy Spirit might pray a perfect prayer through me. I thank You for filling me now to overflowing with the Holy Spirit.

Now you have the power and the tools to win the spiritual battle you are facing. There is still much to learn about skilled warfare and the Holy Spirit will teach you as you are obedient to His direction.

Keep your eyes on Jesus, the Author and Finisher of your faith. Read your Bible daily and ask the Lord to send those who will encourage you and uplift you with the Word of God. And know that the Lord desires reconciliation and wholeness for your marriage and family. Ask Him to help you find a church that believes what God's Word says is true and will stand with you for the healing of your marriage. He is no respecter of persons. What He did for us, He desires to do for you also.

There are ministries dedicated to helping you stand for your marriage. Contact them today.

Covenant Keepers PO Box 702371 Tulsa, OK 74170-2371 covenantkeepersinc.org	Provide support groups, newsletters, tapes and books
Rejoice Ministries PO Box 11242 Pompano Beach, 33061 restored@rejoiceministries.org	Provide email newsletters, tapes and books
Family Foundations Ste 202 1100 W Littleton Blvd Ltttleton, CO 80120 marsha@familyfi.org	Provide seminars, tapes and books